# *The Great Unknown*

## *Musings of the Subconscious*

by

## Farro Kaveh

1

*To my wife, Sue, for her inspiration, and
encouragement.
Without her support, I would not have had the
motivation to take on this new challenge and
bring it to closure.*

## *Acknowledgements*

*I am grateful to Mr. S. Ghotbi for freely sharing
his wisdom and insight into life and the various philosophical
traditions, during our walks in the back streets of Palo Alto.
His review of my poems and constructive encouragement has
been invaluable, and is deeply appreciated.*

*I would like to acknowledge Ms. K. Falandays
of Tell Tell Editing for editing a few of my poems, and for her
helpful comments.*

*I am also thankful to Ms. Suzan Jahangiri, my sister-in-law, for
her support, and help with the editing process.*

*And, last, but not least, I would like to thank Mses. Kristen
Garabadian and Andrea Sandke for the final editing and
formatting of the poems.*

# List of Poems

*Note: the cover and the inside art are originals by the author*

## *Still Life?*

My glasses rest
on the edge of my iPhone,
flutter ever slightly
to the breeze of the ceiling fan.

Nearby the box of tissues
is tempting me to pull out the next tissue,
free it from bondage.

The books and papers strewn on the coffee table
beg me to read them,
but to no avail.

The face in the painting on the wall stares at me,
wondering if I am alive
or another piece of furniture.

The sofa and the rocking chair
invite me to take the weight off my feet,
take it all in
and savor the moment.

The wall clock is ticking away,
oblivious to everything and everyone,
relentless in its singular task,
a cruel reminder of the passage of our lives.

The carpet with its intricate patterns lies before me,
as it has forever, it seems,
giving life to the otherwise barren floor.

The big screen TV is on and has a mind of its own,
sound and images blasting out
into my space,
overwhelming my senses.

The coffee maker is working hard in the background.
The aroma of freshly brewed coffee
permeates the room.

The refrigerator, packed full of stuff,
is humming in the corner,
comforting;
we will not go hungry for long.

All seem to have a purpose,
a clear mission in life,
unlike their creators
who seem to exist
only to exist.

This is the dichotomy of our universe,
the paradox of our lives,
the mystery of our existence.

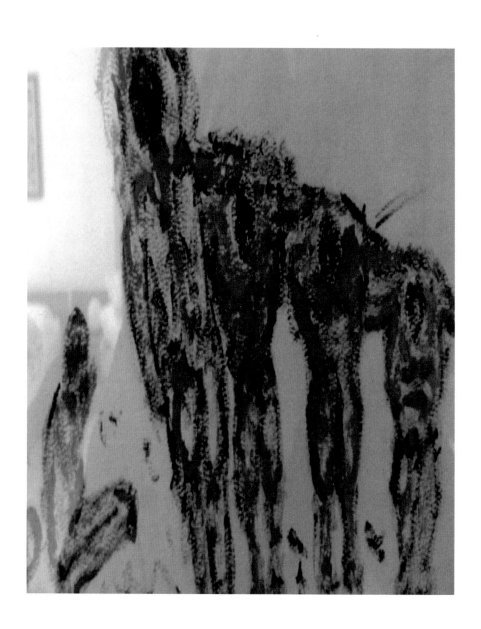

## *The Eternal Mirror*

I am the eternal mirror,
reflecting the ancient lights,
faded images of the distant past,
memories lost in the fog of time.

I reflect what has been,
unforgiving marks of history set deep in my face,
bright lights of promises broken
lost in the furrows of my face.

I am my ancestors,
I am humanity at large,
reflecting the highs and the lows
the triumphs and the failures,
the good and the bad.

The weight of a billion years bears down on me,
the history of mankind echoes from within me,
reverberates, reflects back
into the big void.
Consciousness achieved,
fairy tales spun,
existence romanticized.

I reflect
the conventions set by civilization,
the invented rules,
the intuition bred for millions of years,
the image of the first light
dimmed
by the passage of time.

I carry the light
from the burning bush,
from the earth's core,
from the reflections of the first man,
from the first moonlight shining on that primordial
swamp.

I reflect the light
that came from the Big Bang,
the threshold of creation,
when mankind's destiny was written,
its fate sealed by the elements.

I have stories to tell,
I have wisdom to reveal,
I carry the history of our evolution,
our struggle for perfection,
our struggle to join with our origins,
to close the circle.

I can't help but be true to me,
true to all,
to light up the darkness,
to illuminate the abyss,
guiding the path to a future rooted in the past.

I look straight into the bright lights,
I don't turn away.
I pass on the message
with no hesitation,
no distortion,
for those willing
to listen,
to absorb,
to face the truth.


So heed my message,
don't look away,
face the reality, uncomfortable as it may be.
Salvation is in that
reflected
light.

## *Mithra & the Bull*

I was dreaming last night
that I was flying high,
conversing with the black crows
that perched on the tree of life.

The air was rarefied,
hard to breathe, but easy to fly.
Away and up I went,
then swooped down with a twist.

I heard the sound of waves crashing
on the rocks.
The noise was soothing.
The imagery was supreme.

I closed my eyes,
felt the raindrops on my face.
The air was moist,
heavy with messages.

I let go,
swirled in the wind,
my body twisting and turning.
I looked up and saw a vision
through the mist.

A black hole had opened up,
the universe laid naked,
its secrets
revealed,
its mysteries
in my grasp.

I couldn't believe my good fortune, my salvation.
The wheel of creation at my command.

I turned the wheel.
The horizon bent away,
met the edge of the universe.
The first light appeared.

I sought the light
and flew farther away.
The light changed color.
The wave stretched,
carried me like a cradle.

At a distance I saw the source,
and then it was gone,
changed its position,
created time and space, mass for existence.

I drew closer to see the essence,
the building block.
It hesitated,
turned,
and rushed away with a bang.

I thought:
Is the maestro ashamed of its creation?
Ready to undo what was done?
Close the cycle?
End the expansion?

Or is it me
not able to face reality,
unable to see things as they are:
unfinished,
imperfect,
so much to be desired.

I continued struggling to connect,
to make sense out of the chaos.
The Derik Sea was in turmoil.
I lost my mooring.

I rode on to the field,
changing
in space and time.
My head was spinning,
my brain in overdrive.

I saw the faces of the Great Ones
rushing by, smiling,
giving me
encouragement,
pushing me
to dig deeper.

They had a look of amusement.
They knew the task ahead,
the mystery,
the great unknown,
the slow peeling of the great onion.

I encountered the Higgs bosons flashing by,
weighing on me,
dragging me down,
pulling me
away from the source.

I resisted,
released all the energy I could muster,
connected again,
rode Mithra's Bull
up
and down
into the great unknown.

I saw the cosmic transformation,
creating motion and time,
turning energy into existence,
emptiness into space.

I saw shapes forming,
fractal,
mathematical,
coming to life in different shapes,
life energy
embedded.

I saw my own life flashing by,
gone in a flicker,
so inconsequential.
Energy
to matter,
matter
to life,
life
to dust.

I tried harder to get back to the portal,
to see through the darkness,
see the first light in the distance.

The light flickered,
as if hesitant to shine,
unsure of Genesis,
careful
to a fault,
seeking perfection.

I faced the faint light and smiled,
gave it encouragement,
pursued it to shine,
to spread its energy,
share the miracle.

The light waves began to ebb and flow,
uncertain of their strength,
rising only to fall,
lessons of life
embedded deep within them.

I peered into the light.
The photons raced by,
each holding the secret of creation,
the meaning
of the unknown.

Finally I let go,
succumbed to the pressure,
accepted life as is,
beautiful
in its meaninglessness,
paradoxical in nature.

It brought me freedom, knowing the truth:
no reason for existence,
no mandate to find meaning,
being for the sake of being.

Different from all of creation,
evolution to unknown,
mystery in existence,
challenge to convention.

### The Nonsense That Makes Sense

The nonsense that makes sense,
the disconnection that connects.

Words that have no meaning, yet resonate,
songs of gibberish spawning eloquence.

Mundane objects that cry out substance,
diamond rings that dim the clarity of light.

Stories that go nowhere,
yet lead us to discover our true selves,
works of masters that ring hollow,
conventional.

Everyday lives
that shed light on our existence,
philosophies that spun legends,
yet still fall flat.

Simple truths beyond comprehension,
complexity that mesmerizes,
but feels shallow at the end.

Peasant's admonition going to one's core,
rhythmic poetry that promises salvation,
yet the donkey is dead.

Random words woven together:
sardines, potato chips, Versailles, calligraphy,
an abstract canvas,
a puzzle to be solved.

Musings of an active mind,
breaking free from civilization's noise,
trying to make sense of it all,
uttering words with no apparent meanings.

Following the White Rabbit to the other side,
the answers can be discovered, if one really tries.

Speaking in tongues,
snake charming,
lost in a trance,
breaking free of the norms,
reconnecting to the primordial soup.

Transcending the ordinary,
the conventions set by lineage,
seeing the unvarnished truth for ourselves.

This is the story of us:
confused by our own superficial eloquence,
prisoners of evolution in progress.

## The Gilded Cage

A gilded cage in the wilderness,
far from the primordial soup,
mesmerizing sound of music,
beauty to overwhelm one's senses.

Lives disconnected from the outside,
reality bounded by the golden gates,
civilizations constructed upon myths.

Intellectual pursuits within a fable,
complexities that confuse,
generations untethered from the first light.

Eloquence that demands servitude,
superficiality that deceives,
norms rooted in stories of the past.

Those born in the cage see only the glitter,
are blind to the world beyond,
to the time before the first gate.

They live a life sanctioned generations ago,
when thunder and lightning were of the gods,
Earth was the center of the universe,
and the holy books contained all the answers.

Thin veneer of civilization
was given the golden glow,
eyes made wide open by the glitter.
Jane Austen became a savior,
the haute accent numbed their senses.

Worship of all things beautiful spun new religions,
Man became the center of the universe, the
omnipotent.
Reality moved further from the truth.

Philosophies of existence:
psychotherapy, focus on self, spirituality,
led them further astray.
They forgot their provenance.

Time before the cage was all but forgotten,
became irrelevant, a footnote in their history.

The new construct set them
on a course of detachment.
Everyone became an actor
in this bizarre theater they called life.

The onion of existence was partly peeled,
never to the core,
the truth too strong to face.
Reality was buried in a few layers,
the core was discarded.

Generations lived like orphans,
yearning for their true kin,
only to live an adopted life,
never fully satisfied.

A life unfulfilled grasped
at everything to numb the senses:
religion, wealth, power, war, spirituality,
and entertainment to their heart's delight.

But now the time has come
to break through the gilded gates,
to venture outside, seek the first light,
shed generational dogma.

It is time to reset our history,
burn down the rhetoric,
rein in the self-righteousness,
the self-congratulatory tone,
the celebration of what we have done.

It is time to expose the myths,
the narrative separating us from ourselves,
from the source.
Face the truth.
Seek the first light.

It is time to rewrite our morals,
redefine our heroes,
our measures of success and failure,
what it means to be a human
in search of perfection.

### *Flying in Still Air*

I am flying in the still air,
conferring with the birds,
unburdened by gravity,
free at last from the earthly shackles.

The air is thin, the sun is shining bright.
It gives energy to my body and soul,
my spirit rising beyond my body,
searching for yet higher grounds.

I still can see the people below,
rushing
to nowhere,
their movements appear random,
at times going in circles.
They seem to be chasing their tails.

I can't see the expressions on their faces.
Their voices dissipate in thin air.
Each life's purpose a mystery to me.

Free of all my senses,
oblivious to pain or pleasure,
I feel a deep sense of self-awareness.
My brain is in overdrive.

I smile with a deep sense of satisfaction.
I feel the lightness of my body.
I rise further above the fray.

I begin to believe that I am getting closer to the
origin,
although I know I am so far away,
the illusion soothing – and yet deceiving.

I look up
and seek the great unknown,
the ultimate consciousness,
the key to my existence.

I see the light coming from deep space,
carrying the message of creation,
the spectrum
holding the answer to the eternal puzzle.

I keep looking,
but my eyes are blinded by the light.
I am overwhelmed by this message
from the distant past,
by the burden of history,
the struggles across the ages.

I feel as if I am riding the wave of the elements,
buoyed by dark matter,
floating in the Derik Sea,
cradled like a newborn by a loving parent.

I sense a kinship
to my surroundings.
I am in union with the unseen forces,
feeling the power of the cosmos
running through my body.

I let go of my ego,
my self-consciousness.
I see myself:
one with the universe,
our elements interchangeable,
my thoughts ephemeral,
lost in the vast cosmos.

I leave the earth,
float aimlessly into deep space.
Time seems to be standing still,
gravity waves bending around me,
altering time and space.

I keep on
rising,
leaving
our Milky Way Galaxy,
on the way to a new world.
Feeling the forces unfamiliar,
my consciousness sharpens.
I sense things beyond.

There is a deafening silence around me.
Only a wisp of self remains,
my soul floating
outside of my body.

I think of how the holy books promise
Paradise for the faithful,
and Hell for the non-believers,
of the audience with God or the devil himself.

I wonder if the ancients saw God as light
and the devil as darkness,
as Zarathustra's worship of the eternal flame,
the light for the ages,
fighting darkness
for the salvation of mankind.

But all I see
is a universe engulfed in dark matter.
It seems that the devil is in charge.
The light is desperately fighting
for survival.

The unseen ruling the cosmos,
the apparent world, a small part of the puzzle,
our consciousness vouching for its existence.

I can't tell
if light is the source of my existence,
or dark matter also has a say.
Maybe I will know
if I search
higher,
deeper,
in the space above.

With that in mind,
I let go of my inhibitions.
I move deeper into the great unknown,
I seek what may not be reachable,
that eternal quest
for the hungry souls.

All I feel and see
is emptiness,
the weak and strong forces
fighting for supremacy,
my body
at their mercy.

I begin to ponder my journey to the edge of
knowledge,
my burning desire to find the source of it all,
its essence, its purpose.

I know I am not on a journey of self-discovery,
a quest for self-absorption,
a singular mission for self-indulgence.

I am seeking the essence of existence,
the secret to creation,
the existential matter of existence.

I am to discover the being from nothingness,
the numerals beyond zero,
the unimaginable genesis of existence.

I am seeking the essential truth,
the ultimate knowledge that sets one truly free,
cleansed of dogma and superstition,
of induced nirvana.

I look for guidance from the space above,
from the cosmic guru,
an all-knowing sage,
long lost in the vast cosmos.

Of that life elements reconstituted,
of a billion years of wisdom distilled.
in a singular source,
of an entity who has seen it all.

Of the spirit that envelops the cosmos,
carries the key to creation,
the imponderable source of it all.

I am looking
for that light of enlightenment
coming from deep space.
Elevate me to a higher place,
like that lowly electron yearning
for a higher orbit.

I know the search may be futile,
never-ending,
but the journey is worth taking,
the path lined with eternal peace,
true salvation.

I continue to ascend to the heavens,
hoping for clues,
to set the record straight,
to reset our raison d'être for a meaningful future.

I move closer
to the edge of the universe,
where time has yet to reach,
where all motion comes to a halt,
where matter fights for survival.

Suddenly I realize
the answer is not
in the space above
or anywhere else,
but coded
in the first light long gone,
out of reach,
but perhaps
within reach
through my imagination.

So I turn inwards,
looking for that ultimate clue,
for that marker,
for that link to a billion years past,
for my essential self.

My journey will be long.
I have to peel the onion
of civilization,
of history,
of all the distractions piled on my subconscious.

So
I take the first steps of detachment,
let go of my ego,
look beyond the tip of my nose.

There is vast beauty and trepidation in front of me,
but I am ready to dive in,
go deep inside of myself,
reach
for the ultimate prize.

### The Haze of Rain

Looking through the haze of rain,
the fog is enveloping the ground ahead,
the scenery is surreal,
mesmerizing,
mystical in a sense.

The gray sky seems infinite,
the sound of the light rain
soothing,
breathing life
into the green grass below.

The beauty of the rolling hills
undeniable,
the green color melding into the gray skies,
like a continuum of colors
on a painter's palette.

The scenery is right out of a Van Gogh painting,
waves of brilliant colors
vibrating in space and time,
taking one on a journey of discovery.

A wisp of sunshine
is breaking through the thick clouds,
like an ingénue
peeking through the curtain,
uncertain of what lies ahead.

There is a rainbow forming in the distant hills,
pointing to a pot of gold,
which may – or may not – be there.

The picture changes in an instant.
Clouds disappear.
Full sunshine beams at the welcoming earth,
ready to bathe
in its glow.

The blue sky's dominion over the landscape
gives way
to the lush green fields below,
bright lights surrendering their prime
to a more nuanced hue.

The seemingly inanimate objects
come to life,
orchestrating rays of light
into a symphony of colors of unparalleled beauty.

Everything seems to have its own place on this earth,
each positioned to a certain effect,
to create magic
out of the seemingly ordinary.

The lone oasis
in the barren desert
gives hope of salvation
when all appears lost,
the vast yellow cornfields promise abundance
when the hard work is done.

The green pine trees,
grounded in muddy fields,
pierce the mystical fog,
rise to the heavens above,
salute the invisible,
give shelter to the weary traveler.

The lilies in the fields
move gently in the breeze,
spread their beauty far and wide,
put a pair of young lovers
into a state of euphoria.

The fog
gently rolls in over the green hills,
signals the coming of dusk,
the setting of sun
in the distant hills,
rejuvenating itself
for another day.

And, the last rays of sun
struggle
to illuminate the scenery ahead,
do not give up easily
to the incoming darkness of the night ahead.

I can only be
an observer, lucky
to see the magnificent play of colors unfold
before my eyes,
to see the maestro in action.

42

## *Wonderland*

My mind moves
between reality and the supernatural.
It is in overdrive,
my senses saturated,
my cup overflowing.

I can't control my emotion.
Logic fails me,
science far removed from my consciousness,
fear and emotion in the driver's seat.

I close my eyes to clear my head,
I jump onto the higher ground,
away from the day-to-day noise,
to make sense of my place in the universe.

The struggle is dialectic,
irreconcilable differences at play,
tearing at my soul,
confusion reigning supreme,
I am at the mercy of my DNA.

I try to overcome forces of evolution,
mutate to a higher plane overnight.
My ambition exceeds my ability,
my body and mind failing me.

I try harder,
and suddenly
a sense of clarity permeates my soul.
Peace settles in.
My pulse slows,
my mind is sharp,
ready to receive the faintest signal
from light years past.

I am connecting with the source,
tapping into a sense of purpose,
reason to live –
although it is short-lived,
hard to sustain the moment.
Earth is tugging on my body and soul,
pulling me back to the ground.

I resist, but to no avail,
I lose the connection,
I am back where I started,
petty and small,
neck-deep in the mud of daily existence.

I look out for a sign of true beauty,
for a hint of nobility, higher purpose,
but it is all in short supply,
all tied to personal gain, at all cost,
a zero sum game.

I see the faceless masses
struggling to survive,
the very lucky few,
living in a rarefied space,
free of pain,
feeling above humanity,
demigods amongst the plain mortals.

I look at our ancient institutions:
void of credibility,
under siege by history and science,
facing antipathetic masses,
clinging to their outdated brands.

I fall into despair, lose my sense
of well-being,
hope fades away.
I feel helpless to rise above the mundane;
condemned to live as the human being that I am.

### *The Mirage*

The mirage
has finally turned
into the long-lost oasis,
the dusty haze into water,
the sand into palm trees.

I am quenching my eternal thirst.
My body is resting in the desert shade.

It is now time
to cultivate the fields,
to grow the crop of bounty,
to feed the hungry souls,
to set the wheel of life into motion.

It is time to turn water into sparkling wine,
to get intoxicated,
to spin into a trance,
like a whirling dervish in Konya,
to ascend to the heavens above.

Time to step barefoot onto the burning coal,
to walk calmly on troubled waters,
to soar to the sky like birds of paradise,
to float free
like autumn leaves in the gentle breeze.

Holy Spirit has returned to my body.
My body is my temple.
My mind is at peace,
enlightened,
free at last.

My ideas are becoming reality,
taking shape,
coming alive,
timeless in their beauty.

I have become
the Alchemist,
turning iron into gold.
Miracles abound, barriers fall,
the cosmos opens up.
The light of the universe is coming through.

Am I Lazarus
rising from the dead?
Is the breath of life
permeating my body and soul?
Is this a new beginning,
or is it the end?

Time seems to stop
or start anew,
circle complete,
serpent swallowing its tail,
the crucible of creation in full force.

I savor this moment, as the horizon opens up
and sunlight rises above the distant lands,
illuminating the path to ultimate salvation.

I must seize the moment.
The stars are aligned.
My pulse is synchronized
with the rhythm of the cosmos.
The portal to Paradise has opened,
begging me to cross.

If I hesitate
the moment will be gone,
the waves of opportunity will deconstruct,
the ensuing chaos will cloud the path,
all will be lost, never to be found again.

I charge ahead,
I surrender to the inevitable,
I cross to the other side,
riding the wave of destiny to my ultimate fate.

I have made my peace,
I have done what I came here to do.
Now it is time to let go,
to go
where I was always
destined to go.

## Sheep's Chronicles

Does a sheep have a purpose in life?

Does his life need to have meaning,
have a raison d'être?

Does he feel unfulfilled
when the end comes,
not having grazed all the lush green fields?
Or, does he just take it all on the chin,
and leave this world gracefully?

Does he look back at his life with regret,
or satisfaction,
knowing he did all he could,
and fulfilled his destiny?

Does he wallow in sorrow
for the leaves untouched,
for the green grass wasted?
Or does he simply accept his fate,
at peace with the many leaves unturned?

Does he get depressed
and have a midlife crisis,
or
is he an eternal optimist
with no down days?

Does he look at other sheep with disdain,
or share the grassy steppes,
revel in camaraderie,
cherish his flock?

Does he think about sheep in other countries,
and curse the fate of his geography?
Or does he roam in his green fields, satisfied?

Does he look with envy at humans
with their opposable thumbs and peculiarities
or does he just shake his head,
and bleat aloud in disbelief?

Does he imagine a creator,
and worship His being,
or does he plough through life
oblivious to a creator,
take things as they come?

Does he have consciousness,
awareness of his existence?
Or is he all flesh,
with a minimum of an instruction set
locked in his DNA?

Does he have deep thoughts about life
and his place in the universe,
or does he just graze along,
take in the scenery,
and thank evolution for his good fortune?

Does he represent evolution at its finest,
or is he an evolutionary failure,
meat for the hungry hordes?

Does he feel any intimacy
with his parents and offspring,
or he is all for himself,
alone in this world?

Does he make any friends
with fellow grazers,
or he is a loner,
pondering his existence?

Is he a role model for us humans,
searching for meaning,
where none is to be had?
Or does he shun us?
Does he see us as not worthy of his attention?

I say, let the sheep be our model to live by,
unsophisticated, free of dogma and superstition,
with no need for meaning in life,
an accident of creation,
a blessing in disguise.

Let us celebrate our being,
the unlikely probability of our existence,
nothing more,
nothing less,
doing our best to sort things out.

54

## The Wind

The wind showed up
uninvited at our doorstep.
We didn't know where it came from,
where it was headed;
likely to the open fields,
where the sunflowers grow.

Let the wind blow,
let it howl,
let it stir up the leaves,
rush through the winding alleys
of that old village with mud brick walls.

Let it blow over the deep blue sea,
create the ripples that ever so gently
kiss the sandy beach,
or the roaring waves that crash against
the mighty rocks blocking its way.

Don't try to catch it.
Don't stand in its way,
or kill its spirit,
its desire to roam free,
to caress everything in its path.

Don't stand in its way.
Let it be.
Let it find its way.
Let it scream
as it struggles through the dark alleys,
let it take a deep sigh of relief
when it reaches
the open field.

Let the wind blow.
Let it carry the messages of our ancestors,
the voices of the voiceless,
the songs of liberation,
the chants of ecstasy from the distant shores.

Listen
intensely.
Let the message resonate, amplify in your mind,
like a twister in the desolate desert,
capturing energy from the still air,
and then releasing it back into the vast unknown.

The story of the wind
is the story of humanity:
seeking equilibrium, peace, and tranquility,
to be left alone,
free to find our own path.

The wind has no regrets,
does not look back.
It speeds through confined spaces,
lingers in the wide open spaces,
takes it all in.

Let the wind blow,
let it wipe the slate of history clean,
rewrite what it means to be human,
to become worthy
of billions of years of struggle for perfection.

Let it erase our sins,
our indiscretions,
our history of ignorance,
our hypocrisy,
our insanity,
our cruelty,
our pettiness.

Let the wind bring us peace,
a sense of dignity.
Let it be our model to live by.

Take heed of its capacity to change,
to adapt,
and mold things in its path.

58

### *Almighty Algebra*

Life is mathematical, may be statistical,
in a way magical,
made in the image of almighty algebra.

Physics is mathematics, Nature's laws,
all the same, all reduced to numbers,
the invention of a master mathematician.

The master mathematician sitting at the table of
creation,
setting universe in motion,
motion to time,
life to evolution.

Writing equations to map our universe,
to govern our daily lives,
setting boundaries on our existence.

Pulse of the heart,
leaves on the trees,
all fractals.
Follow the numbers,
there lies the reason for our existence.

It all adds up,
from the infinitesimal to infinity,
in an instant,
with a big bang,
artifact of a singularity.

Are all things accumulative? you wonder.
Matter? Life itself?
There are magical numbers,
guiding us in unseen ways.

Years, one's life, linear, exponential,
depending on circumstance.
Feelings add, subtract,
leaving us fulfilled
or in a void.

The speed of light is a constant through the ages,
carrying the secret of our universe,
never wavering, always moving.

Age of the universe, the first light,
the speed of light, reduced to numbers,
simple, to the point,
following basic mathematics.

Electrons and protons
add up
to a balanced charge,
stability,
covalent bonds searching for perfection,
filling in the voids,
making matter that matters.

Two ears, two eyes, five fingers, and not six,
the magic of evolution,
optimization problem solved,
efficiency of purpose evident.

Entropy,
unidirectional,
accumulative,
pointing to infinity,
the end in sight –
or a billion years away.

Subtract the identical, left with nothing,
void defined, diversity key to existence,
the magical essence of creation.

Snowflakes,
each different at a closer look,
tell the story:
creation's random numbers generator at its best.

Evolution:
sum of changes through the ages,
always adding or subtracting,
like the crust of the earth,
layers on top of layers.

Find the meaning of zero,
find the key to creation,
subtraction key to transformation,
motion subtraction of matter
in time and space.

Addition nothing but subtraction,
nothing created,
nothing destroyed,
each addition, balanced by a subtraction.


So take heed of the numbers,
our first expression of consciousness;
that is where we all started,
that is where it all ends.

### The Bird and the Seed

I am that bird
that flies
from one tree to another.
I am that seed
that grows into a willow tree,
giving shade to the weary traveler.

I am that dog in the yard
that runs
from one end to the other,
seemingly without reason.
I am that wanderer who is searching
for the meaning of it all.

I am that light
that travels
from the distant suns
to give sight
to the millions lost in their ways.
I am that wind
that blows the dust away,
revealing the great unknown.

I am that song
that echoes in your head,
the source unknown, the purpose evident.
I am
that mesmerizing music
that never ends.

I am that meteor that brings life to the planets.
I am that sage with the hidden message
for those who want to listen.

I am that sand that holds duality of purpose.
I am that mythical alchemist
turning iron into gold,
breaking old bonds,
forging them anew.

I am that force that holds
the universe in balance.
I am that whirling dervish
on the verge of ecstasy,
leaving this world behind.

I am that surging wave,
cheered on by the distant wind.
I am that luminous
falling
leaf,
twirling aimlessly in the autumn breeze.

I am that field of yellow sunflowers,
captured in a seminal painting.
I am the black crows descending,
oblivious to the menacing scarecrow.

I am that ocean wave
holding
the essence of life.
I am that mighty cliff,
weathered
and battered
but still
standing tall.

I am that dark matter,
engulfing the universe,
unseen but ever present,
bending gravity waves at will,
remaining in the background.

I am that outsize ego,
God's gift to humanity.
I am that humble soul,
changing the world in unseen ways.

I am that puzzle that begs to be solved.
I am that enigma that is hard to crack.
I am the mystery of life.
I am the simplicity of the obvious.

I am the madness that is universal,
I am the sanity that is in short supply,
the sun that peeks through the cloud,
reaching for an audience with the sunflower.

I am the wisdom of the cosmos,
embedded in our genes.
I am
as insignificant as
the pebble on the beach,
yet omnipresent in the universe.

I am the all-knowing seer,
master of the mystery.
I am the key to our survival.
I am hopelessly lost in the desert of life,
searching for an oasis of existence.

I am the artisan, on the verge
of creating my opus magnum.
I am the distracted failed soul,
looking for meaning in my life.

I am the flowing stream,
murmuring my way to the crystal clear lake.
I am the rush of muddy water,
flooding the once-dry creek.
I am you.
You are me.
I am everything,
and I am nothing,
free as the void,
burdened as the mountain's base,
tall as the cedar tree,
yet humble as the willow tree.

I am the lonely traveler
on the dusty road to salvation,
I am the bewildered soul in the
maddening crowd, lost in the moment,
all my senses in overdrive.

I am the consummate connoisseur
of the sophisticated,
I am the shallow consumer of the mundane,
easily distracted by the bright lights.

I am a contradiction, a hypocrite at best.
I am just a human, a slave to my genes,
a billion years of evolution
crammed into one finite life.

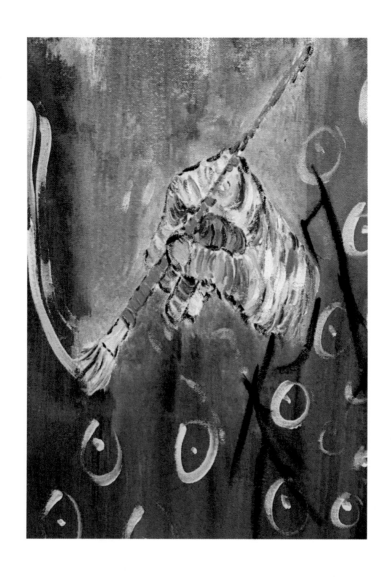

### *Connecting the Dots*

I see the world explode
in my mind's eye
into a billion pieces,
a pointillist's canvas
stretching across the universe,
a perfect composition:
all balanced, all parts in harmony.

I see a vast palette of magnificent colors,
bright lights of infinite depth,
conceived in the Big Bang,
tempered through the ages.

I see clouds of particles
weaving the tapestry of life in the distance,
with every hidden stroke
a magical picture emerges from the darkness.

The beauty is breathtaking,
the energy supreme,
the will to change, expand into the void evident,
creating space-time along the way.

The cosmic dance is in full display,
a ballet
choreographed by the great unknown,
mesmerizing in its beauty,
difficult to fathom.

The improvisation is awe-inspiring:
creativity at its core.
The force within cannot be denied,
molding the universe in its image.

Unseen forces bond, tear matter apart,
all in action and reaction,
seeking
equilibrium,
perfection,
immortality.

The order in chaos is self-evident,
dichotomy of universe,
duality of nature
present
at the core of creation,
manifested in our own being.

Matter and anti-matter,
charges positive and negative,
good and evil,
all balance out,
nothing destroyed, nothing created,
mystery of creation unresolved.

I see the bright stars, destroyed into black holes:
darkness engulfing light,
no escaping from evil,
like so many bright lights extinguished before their time.

I search for the origin in the chaos.
Heisenberg uncertainty leads me astray,
lost between worlds
that may
or may not
exist.

I go back in my mind
billions of years in a flash.
I see a glimpse of the beginning,
but
my imagination stops at the margins.

I feel the consciousness of the universe,
the beating heart of the cosmos,
setting in motion waves of creation,
as frequent as light itself.

I see the rise and fall of light waves,
echoing the ebb and flow of life,
deep within the eternal space.

Crossing zero for nonexistence,
peaks on either side, opposites,
reflecting light and darkness,
as in the cycles of our days.

There seems to be
no beginning
and no end.
The cycle repeats,
as with that coiled spring,
bursting out of the dusty old box in the attic.

74

## Upside Down

In this world
images are upside down,
rules are in reverse,
conventions are set on their heads.

People walk backwards.
Birds fall from the sky.
The earth drifts away from itself.
Cows float
above green fields,
weightless.

Darkness begins the day
and the sun rises in the west,
comes on with a blast of darkness.
The moon takes center stage in the western skies.

Mirrors devour the light.
Images reflect back from dark crevasses.
Rainbows are cast in barren deserts.

Tree roots are suspended in the air.
Flowers bend towards darkness,
shy away from the bright lights.

The sky looks hollow.
Earth's core bellows above,
red lava oozing out from the sky.

Sunrays freeze unsuspecting souls.
Polar ice is steaming hot, boils the ocean,
rainforests are starved for even one drop of rain.

The stormy oceans offer tranquility to weary travelers,
and the calm seas are a source of anxiety and anguish.

The scarecrow
Welcomes
descending crows with open arms.
The sunflower fields
shun the bright light of the sun.

The fish fly uninhibited in the sky,
the fishermen chasing them in midair,
anglers aimlessly searching the skies.

Nightingales sound ominous,
and the crows soothe the anxious souls,
sing songs of ecstasy in the evening hours.

The wind calms stormy seas,
a summer breeze wreaks havoc in the prairies,
upends the cornfields.

In this world
dirt is the valued commodity.
Gold is treated like dirt,
people hoard garbage,
mansions are erected from refuse.

The clowns preach from the pulpit,
men of good faith do cartwheels in the circus,
and the crowd roots for the piranha.

The faithful
burn
crosses
in their neighbors' front yards,
sing
hateful hymns from the holy books,
praise the lord
under their breaths.

Books are fodder for the bonfire of ignorance,
gossip and junk news rule the airways,
shaming the innocents an arena sport.

The lowly rat is the king of the jungle.
The mighty lion cowers in the corner.
The snake in the grass is the kingmaker.

For every action
there is no reaction.
Water flows up to the snowy peaks.
Frogs sing hallelujah in unison.

In this world
evolution is recessive,
intelligence in short supply,
false idols worshipped by the masses.

People line up to bow before the latest gadgets,
holy marketers stir up the masses,
apps are the keys to eternal salvation.

Peacemakers are busy waging wars.
Warmongers preach the gospel of brotherly love.
Red roses sprout from cold gun barrels.

Gods prance pompously in the streets,
disdain the downtrodden
and praise
the vulgar,
the despicable souls.
The devil looks on in shock.

The search for the meaning of life
is the eternal joke.
Superstition and dogma trump reason,
hatred of the other
sold as food for the soul.

The bigger the lie the more palatable.
Truth is in short supply,
hoopla and bravado the norm,
humility a mortal sin.


This
is the world they have created
in their dreams,
now busy making it come alive,
thought to matter,
matter to life,
transformation complete.

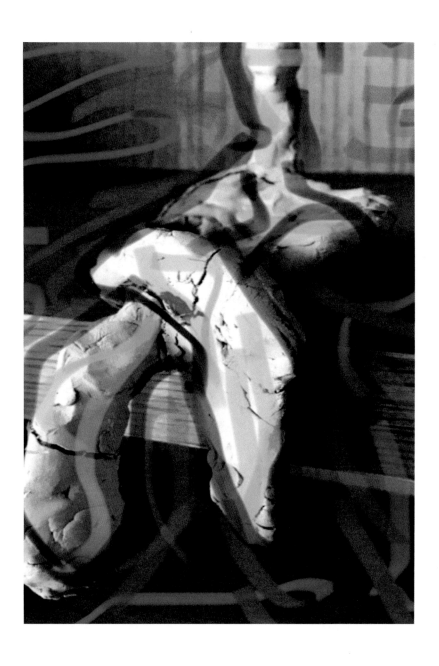

80

### La Dolce Vita?


You know your wine,
you read the classics,
have an eye for all things sophisticated,
the seemingly unreachable.

You engage in uppity talk.
You quote the greats with authority,
pause to adjust your fancy shades,
run your hand through your thick head of hair.

You sip on that expensive wine,
partake in the casual conversation,
impress the glitterati with your intellect,
your utter worldliness.

You get on that one-hundred-foot yacht in
St. Tropez with grace,
dazzle the jet set with your wit,
disarm them with your infectious charm.

Your presence on the court is an event,
your elegant backhand
sends shivers down the ladies' spines,
your sip on that gin and tonic cause for
an orgasm.

You do all of this with seemingly no effort,
breeze through life on cruise control,
take in the scenery,
give nothing back in return.

You dabble in the arts.
You play a nasty tune on the piano,
recite T.S. Eliot's *Wasteland* in a snap,
everything well-rehearsed,
tastefully choreographed.

You see life as a theater,
yourself the main protagonist,
the rest of us, your adoring fans,
clamoring for your attention.

You are called
a renaissance man,
connoisseur of style,
a man for all seasons,
the envy of your peers.

You revel in the flattery,
you up the ante every day,
leave your imitators in the dust.

You live this life as the ultimate in sophistication,
evolved genteel man,
and to the end,
with panache and flair.

You never hesitate in your beliefs, your way of life.
A skillful actor you are in the theater of life.

You never question your life's purpose,
your place in the universe.
You follow the conventions set by the élites.

Your life
is a quintessential good life,
rich in texture,
full of color and vibe.

You do not think of the afterlife,
or the end,
when the Pied Piper strides into town.

You are game until the end
slip into eternity with grace,
with your wry smile still on your face.


Your epitaph will read:
He came,
he enjoyed life,
he left nothing behind,
not even crumbs for the rest of us.

### *Ordinary Man*

He was an ordinary man,
with average tastes, average ambitions.
He did not
stand out
from the crowd.

His life's mission was to be ordinary,
lost in average statistics,
never
on either tail of the curve.

His ordinary life disguised his keen intellect,
his demeanor professed his humility,
his desire to be average,
anonymous to the end.

He never spoke out in the crowd,
content to listen,
to keep his opinions to himself.
He laughed at all jokes,
nodded his head at all absurdities.

He hardly engaged in any serious discussions,
excused himself from all matters of contention.

He constantly disappointed
his superiors,
since by all accounts he looked the part,
but did not play the game,
stayed out of the limelight.

He stood on the sidelines,
happy to be the second fiddle,
to work in the background,
never the front man.

He chuckled at his Alpha male friends,
never enticed to join their club,
to play the high-stakes game of one-upmanship.

His favorite musical acts
were the backup singers, singing in the dark,
never stepping into center stage,
always the supporting cast.

He was well-liked by all,
no threat to their ego,
their sense of self-importance,
made everybody feel good about themselves.

He was once an ambitious kid
who easily stood out from the crowd,
with little effort or mischief.

His good looks, athletic prowess,
and high intelligence, were difficult to ignore,
a source of both envy and pride.

Slowly he began to downplay his virtues,
to blend in with the crowd,
become one of them,
average to the end.

He disposed of all pretensions,
was as straight as an arrow,
religiously protected his soul from corruption, from
all servitude.

He did not play any games.
He was honest to the core,
apolitical as they come, some say naive,
seemingly gullible.

He did not aspire for a legacy to speak of,
to write books about,
no myths to propagate,
just a nondescript life, ordinary as they come.

This did not bother him a bit.
He was not motivated by a legacy,
by his impact on society at large.
He saw the world through a different lens.

He did not believe in all the brouhaha,
the grandstanding, the triumphs and failures.
He saw them as nothing lasting,
of no eventual consequence.

He saw all events as ultimately ephemeral,
all emotions fleeting,
all things temporary,
all legacies at the end
immaterial,
fading in due time.


He was, after all, an ordinary man,
leading an ordinary life,
reveling in ordinary rituals,
content to slip away
unnoticed,
ashes to ashes,
dust to dust.

90

## The Last Supper

I was in a deep dream,
dining with the greatest painters of the
last millennia,
saluting them with a drink or two.

It was as if it were the Last Supper:
one last chance for all to be present,
to see the others' perspectives,
to hear each unique world view.

I had the power to see inside their minds,
to read their deepest thoughts, feel their passion,
know their raison d'être.

Their egos manifest, their souls laid open,
their genius on full display,
their inquisitive eyes revealing their stories,
their desires.

Each had seen the word differently,
created new realities, set new conventions,
changed the course of civilization,
our understanding of the world.

Picasso was in a heated debate with Leonardo,
their Mona Lisas face to face,
each claiming the mantle of beauty.

Generations separated them,
so much difference,
yet so similar,
each within them a hidden message.

Van Gogh reaching for a loaf of bread,
overheard the conversation,
presented a third form,
waves of melancholy from his brush
telling a different tale.

Michelangelo, standing above Da Vinci
with his imposing figure,
was leaning against the marble wall,
anxious to show off his genius,
to claim the mantle of ultimate creativity.

El Greco, ahead of his time,
seemed out of place,
gazing into the distance where images
seem more slender, reaching for the sky,
for the heavens above.

Dali, unfazed by the gravity of the moment,
was playful, took his time to enjoy the scene,
imagined it as only he would, surrealistic,
a fanciful play on reality.

Kandinsky was amused by all the fuss.
He saw art as an abstraction of the real world,
of tangled images, of a puzzle to be deciphered,
the public as participants, the ultimate arbiters.

Creation their choice, their sense of beauty, their prerogative,
each looking and seeing something different,
original in their visions, visionary in their origins.

They all saw reality not as a simple construct;
relativity written all over it,
all in the eyes of the beholder,
created to one's delight,
making life bearable,
worth the next breath.

One created beauty to please a master,
the other to rebel against convention,
and yet one to release his anxiety,
his art his reason to live.

Each brush stroke telling so many stories,
the decision to go up or down, short or long,
within them their judgement, their fate,
a sense of finality, acceptance of the end.

Would we still talk about Mona Lisa
if her lips were not
ever so slightly turned up?
Or is it the mischievous smile
that makes it a masterpiece,
captures our hearts, our imaginations?

No one ever knows.
Once created, it is done,
it is what it is, open for all to see, to judge,
the painter's soul laid bare.

We each see
what we want in the images,
love or hate the master's work,
draw our own conclusions,
make up our own minds.

It is like creation itself.
Once unleashed it takes on a life of its own,
its meaning
for us to interpret,
its mysteries to be solved.

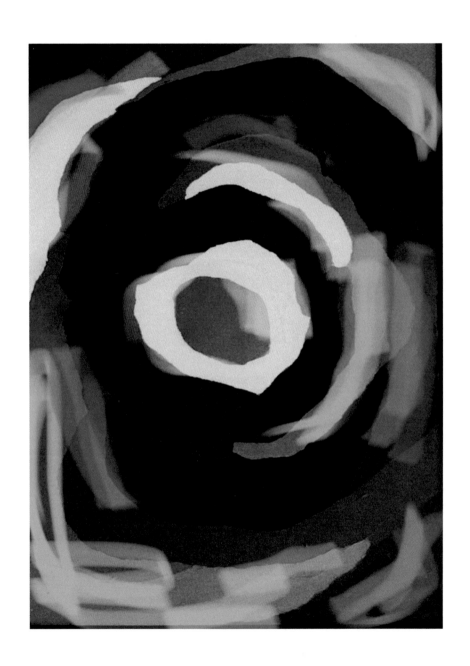

## *From a Distance*

From a distance
colors fade, fuse together,
images blur,
distinctions disappear.

All things become small, insignificant.
We see patterns, not individual things.

Objects appear to stand still,
mirages form,
existence becomes tentative, questionable,
things fade into the background.

Sounds lose distinction.
Oration is lost in white noise, turns abstract.
Certainty and dogma disappear.
Tranquility sets in.

Our senses coalesce,
our minds clear,
our thoughts become crisp,
free from the interference of sound and images.

We become color blind, see only shapes of humanity,
silhouettes blending in with the background.

Earthly norms and conventions dissolve into ether.
New rules emerge out of the vacuum,
in harmony with the cosmos.

We become one with the universe.
Truth reveals itself.
Life's meaning is made apparent.

We move to a higher plateau of existence,
our physical bodies become our souls.
Pain is replaced with joy,
envy with sympathy,
hatred with love.

The forces of proximity give way
to the pull of the planets near and far,
dark energy in competition with gravity.
We get lost within the elements,
buoyed by unseen forces,
cradled by light from the distant past.

We see ourselves
as one with the others,
separated only by forces unseen,
preferences temporary,
alliances fleeting.

We are, after all, organized into a being without consent,
separate ourselves by force of will,
only to join the origin
again
at the end.

Our composition a temporary construct,
of unsustainable complexity to be simplified,
and left to the passage of time.

100

## The Child Within

Welcome to reality, my old friend.
Where have you been?
Are you ready to come face to face with yourself?

Welcome to the hall of a thousand mirrors,
where reflections rule.
No escaping reality;
you are trapped, nowhere to hide.

Welcome to the world of bright lights and
dark shadows,
of reflections,
of a thousand speculations.

The world of virtual images, seemingly real,
of reality caught off-guard,
hanging in the open space, for all to see.

The world of left being right,
and right to your left,
the world of eyes wide open,
looking straight back with no mercy,
no hesitations.

Welcome, my friend.
Are you ready to face the truth,
look directly into your own eyes,
face reality, accept who you are?

There is nowhere to turn,
no corners to hide behind.
Everything is laid bare.
Time to come clean,
face your demons.

This is your chance to absorb the light,
to shed the darkness,
to clear the dark passages,
to reflect the bright lights back from within
and illuminate the world.

You have hidden behind a façade for too long,
the *bal masqué* has long come and gone.
It is time to come clean.

As painful as it may be,
this is your chance
to confess,
to tell the whole world
of your pettiness,
of your indiscretions,
of the righteous path not taken,
the road to self-destruction,
of opportunities lost.

This is how you are set free,
liberated from within,
how you find peace at last.

A new beginning beckons,
Reincarnation
in this lifetime,
nirvana
at last.

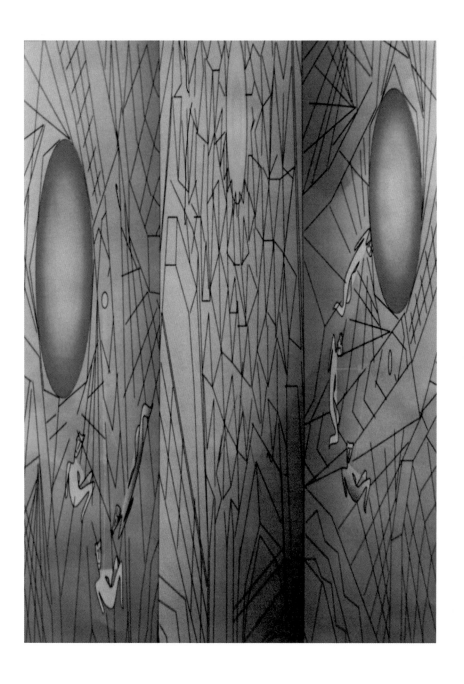

### *Clouds of Consciousness*

I am hovering over the crowd.
Am I awake or in a dream?
I see everyone as they truly are.

Everywhere I look I see swirling clouds,
electrons circling
protons and neutrons,
photons streaming with the speed of light.
What a mesmerizing sight to behold!

Clusters of particles move at dizzying speeds,
at times embracing,
at times rejecting,
digging in,
attaching,
detaching,
moving on.

The particles move in mysterious ways,
seemingly controlled by unknown forces
emanating from the clouds, channeling through,
initiating new clouds,
forming new imagery.

New clusters form from other clusters,
organizing particles into different shapes,
giving them new life, new direction.

Consciousness passes from one cloud to another,
sound waves of particles, photons,
bouncing off dense clouds.

With seemingly subtle movements,
reflecting waves of photons rush
to clouds of carbon particles,
eager to receive the energy,
to transform, contort, reorganize.

Energy is absorbed,
the glow of long-wave particles is reflected back,
bursts of movements in the clouds ensue.

Other carbon clusters react on cue,
swirl in unison, generate a rhapsody of colors,
like a pointillist landscape unfolding before our eyes.

The connection is infinite,
traversing the cosmos,
uniting galaxies, worlds beyond,
all part of the same construct,
with no boundary.

The continuum of matter and energy
expands outward
claiming space and time,
where before there were none,
lay opportunity for other worlds to come forth,
create new realities.

We are
an infinitesimal part of this universe,
yet we are
the sole observers,
the sole arbiters of reality,
mediators of cosmic forces fighting for supremacy.

## The End

It comes suddenly, often with no warning,
with no rhyme, nor reason.

Some movies end with a fade to black,
some with a bang,
yet, questions always remain.

Closure is rarely a fait accompli,
possibilities abound,
the most obvious, rarely the answer.

A boulder will roll down the mountain,
where, and when it rests, never a certainty,
never foretold.

As it is with our lives,
our destiny unknown, never set in stone;
we, the wanderers in the winding alleys
of that ancient bazaar.


The end is always the hardest,
like the last brush stroke on a canvas;
finality is the art of the magi,
the purview of the sage.

Made in the USA
San Bernardino, CA
28 July 2020